Original title:
A Walk Through Paradise

Copyright © 2025 Creative Arts Management OÜ
All rights reserved.

Author: Jasper Montgomery
ISBN HARDBACK: 978-1-80581-665-2
ISBN PAPERBACK: 978-1-80581-192-3
ISBN EBOOK: 978-1-80581-665-2

Tranquil Journeys Through Natural Havens

In fields of daisies, I trip on a bee,
The buzzing dance makes me swap my tea.
I wave at the clouds, they wave back with rain,
"I just wanted sunshine!" I curse in vain.

A squirrel steals my sandwich, he looks quite sly,
As I chase him down, I feel like I fly.
The breeze plays tricks, my hat takes a dive,
Now it's a game, can I survive?

Light and Shadow Among the Bloom

In gardens where laughter and daisies collide,
A ladybug lands on my nose, what a ride!
I try to impress by doing a jig,
But slip on a petal, what fun to be big!

Bunnies in shades wearing shades of their own,
While gossiping flowers turn green with a groan.
They whisper and giggle, their petals all sway,
While I start to wonder if I'm in their play.

Celestial Pathways of Joy

With stars in my pockets, I stroll in the night,
Chasing my shadow, oh what a fright!
A comet zooms past to give me a scare,
I laugh as I duck, then pull out my hair.

Moonbeams are giggling, they tickle my feet,
While crickets all chirp to a silly beat.
I dance with the fireflies, oh what a sight,
Who knew that my shoes would take off in flight!

Glimmers in the Twilight Grove

In the twilight grove, oh what a sight,
Squirrels in tuxedos, dancing with delight.
They twirl and spin, on branches so high,
While raccoons applaud with pies in the sky.

A hedgehog juggles acorns with ease,
While owls exchange jokes, oh such a tease!
Fireflies flash, in a playful chase,
As frogs on lily pads try to keep pace.

The trees lean closer to hear the show,
While a fox in a top hat steals the glow.
In this whimsical place where laughter roams,
The twilight grove hums with cheerful tones.

Riding the Winds of Serendipity

On a breeze of giggles, I take to the skies,
With ducks on skateboards and surprising goodbyes.
A parrot in shades, whistling a tune,
While clouds play hopscotch under the moon.

Balloons chat sweetly, like old friends do,
While balloons wear stripes in bright yellow and blue.
A raccoon with a map claims he's quite lost,
But finds his way home by following toast.

The sun winks kindly, like an old chap,
As a turtle on rollerblades takes a nap.
With laughter and whimsy, the winds do peak,
On a ride of chance, we all feel unique.

Shades of Grace Beyond the Horizon

At dusk times grace, where colors collide,
A snail wears a cape, takes his time with pride.
Butterflies gossip about the day's grime,
While clouds share tales of the silliest crime.

The sun bows low with a twinkle and cheer,
While daisies burst forth, singing loud and clear.
A llama in shades prances by the fence,
With a hoot and a holler, oh what a tense!

Leaves in the breeze play tag with the night,
And fireflies join in, glowing just right.
In a realm of goofy sights untold,
Where laughter lives, and hearts are bold.

The Song of Infinite Meadows

In the meadows vast, a chorus begins,
With bunnies on tambourines making spins.
Fluffy clouds giggle, drifting about,
As daisies all dance, swaying without doubt.

A hedgehog conducts with style and flair,
While crickets provide rhythm, a musical pair.
Pigs in sunglasses play hopscotch and cheer,
In this endless meadow, there's plenty to hear.

The stream hums along with a bubbly sound,
As frogs in tuxedos leap 'round and 'round.
Nature's own symphony, made up of fun,
In a world full of laughter, just bursting with sun.

Delights of the Sun-Drenched Glade

Bouncing bunnies hop and prance,
Chasing shadows in a dance.
Squirrels juggling acorns high,
Witty birds with a gossiping sigh.

In this glade where laughter roams,
Even frogs are crafting poems.
A picnicking bear steals a pie,
While wise old owls just wonder why.

Soft Murmurs of the Blooming Vale

Tulips gossip, petal to petal,
While daffodils argue over a medal.
Bees in tuxedos dance just right,
As ants throw a surprise night flight.

A bunny who's mastering hopscotch,
Wearing a hat that's rather botch.
This vale blossoms with laughter's stir,
As flowers tease, 'What's that on her fur?'

Colors of Utopian Mornings

Crisp sunrises on painted skies,
Where pickle jars hold firefly spies.
Rainbow socks for the morning breeze,
And chocolate milk fills all our teas.

Frogs singing tunes from a hit parade,
Dancing in their leafy brigade.
The sun yawning, stretching wide,
As giggling clouds begin to glide.

The Secret Sanctuary of Dreams

In a nook where laughter dwells,
Pillow fights and tinkling bells.
A gnome tries to juggle some cheese,
While kittens play tag with the bees.

Cloud monsters revel in shadowy play,
Tickling the stars at the end of the day.
Dreams are silly, full of cheer,
With hiccuping rainbows, oh so dear!

Strolls Among Starlit Blossoms

In the garden, flowers dance,
Chasing shadows with a glance.
Worms wear hats, they twirl in glee,
Sipping nectar like it's tea.

Butterflies don silly shades,
Swapping jokes in leafy glades.
Bees buzz by, they can't be late,
Arriving just to celebrate.

Trees share tales of grassy games,
While petals giggle with strange names.
The moon laughs loud, a cosmic cheer,
As crickets strum their banjo near.

A squirrel dressed in polka dots,
Plays hopscotch on the spots.
Every step, a laugh-filled quest,
In this place, we jest the best.

Whispering Breezes of Eden

Wind whispers secrets, soft and light,
Worms in ties take flight at night.
Frogs in tuxedos croak a tune,
Underneath a glowing moon.

Blades of grass roll in a race,
While daisies giggle, "What a place!"
Every breeze, a cheeky prank,
Puffing clouds, the whole sky sank.

The sun wears shades, conspires too,
With cheeky squirrels playing peekaboo.
Every petal's throw confetti,
As the world spins, never petty.

Laughter leaks through hedgerows tight,
In this Eden, all feels right.
Wandering on, I can't dismiss,
This garden's bliss, a comical twist.

Footsteps on Celestial Soil

On celestial paths, we trip and fall,
Chasing laughter that's heard by all.
Clouds form shapes of silly clowns,
And sprinkle joy through flowery towns.

Stars peek down with twinkling grins,
While frogs in flippers take a spin.
Every step a little slip,
Oh! Watch out for that comet's dip!

Dancing daisies, what a sight,
Invite the moon to join their flight.
Marigolds wear bubblegum hats,
Playing games with friendly cats.

In this realm, humor's the key,
With every giggle, we're all free.
Step by step, our hearts will soar,
In this paradise, who could ask for more?

The Garden of Eternal Dreams

In dreams we wander, quite absurd,
With talking plants that sing unheard.
Jellybeans grow on candy trees,
While honeybees sip root beer teas.

Gnomes on unicycles race,
Chasing butterflies in a chase.
Each flower winks with playful might,
Daring the sun to join their fight.

Light bulbs swing from rainbow vines,
Tickling the clouds until they shine.
Whimsical wind, a jester's tune,
Leaves us laughing 'neath the moon.

In this garden, dreams take flight,
With every turn, a comic sight.
Here, joy's the fruit that we both seek,
As laughter echoes, cheeky and unique.

Traces of the Whispering Woods

In the woods where squirrels dance,
Even trees seem to wear pants.
Birds gossip with the buzzing bees,
While mushrooms giggle in the breeze.

A rabbit hops in shoes too tight,
Chasing shadows, what a sight!
The branches wave, a friendly tease,
As secrets rustle through the leaves.

A raccoon winks with snacks he stole,
He shares his treats and tells a joke.
Every twig holds tales so grand,
With whispers from the forest band.

So tiptoe lightly, hold your breath,
In this place where joy won't rest.
The woods will tickle, giggles soar,
And leave you wanting to explore.

Dreamcatcher's Expedition

On a quest for dreams, what a ride,
With pillows soft and ducks that glide.
We bounce through clouds, land on a star,
With pajamas on, we go so far.

Tickle the trees, they start to laugh,
Watch a cat who thinks it's a giraffe.
With kernels of corn that giggle and pop,
We'll dance through rainbows, never stop.

Chasing wild dreams like fluffy bees,
We trip on clouds, oh what a tease!
Laughter echoing in air so sweet,
As merry-go-rounds skip to our beat.

So grab your dreams, let's sail away,
In this land where we can play.
Throw away worry, let joy inside,
On this ride of dreams, let's glide!

Fragrance of the Fabled Garden

In the garden where flowers sing,
Petunias belt out their bling-bling.
With daisies plotting a dance-off spree,
And roses bragging, "Look at me!"

A sunflower dons a wacky hat,
While bunnies debate on who's more fat.
Butterflies flipping like acrobats,
Making giggly plans with fuzzy rats.

Tomatoes chuckle, ripe and round,
As pumpkins do flips, spring off the ground.
The garden blooms with giggling cheer,
Every petal whispers secrets near.

So wander here, miss not a giggle,
In this place where flowers wiggle.
With scents of fun in each soft breeze,
Join the laughter with such ease!

Delight Under the Azure Sky

Beneath the blue, where seagulls squawk,
We sip on juice and take a walk.
The sun winks down with a cheeky grin,
As flip-flops dance, let fun begin.

A dog in shades steals all the show,
While children toss ice cream, watch it go.
Kites are tangled, it's a glorious mess,
Life here feels like a silly dress.

On the beach, we build castles high,
With whimsy waves that wave goodbye.
The sandy shores, a canvas bright,
Where laughter paints the day's delight.

As sunset hues begin to blend,
We laugh and play until the end.
In moments like these, joy won't conceal,
Under this sky, every heart can heal.

Pathways of Glowing Petals

In gardens where the daisies play,
The ants have all learned how to sway.
With petals bright as candy floss,
They giggle as they toss and toss.

Bumblebees hum a silly tune,
While butterflies dance 'neath the moon.
Each step is filled with joyous glee,
As squirrels act out a comedy.

The flowers tease, they tickle too,
They whisper secrets just to you.
Blowing kisses from the breeze,
As frogs jump in, attempting ease.

But watch your step, or you might trip,
On daisies that laugh and flip.
In this place where joy will bloom,
You can't help but feel the room!

Laughter Among the Lilies

Underneath a sky so bright,
Where daisies giggle with delight.
The lilies wear their silly hats,
As turtles joke with chubby rats.

In shades of green, the grasswaves sway,
While frogs declare it's 'Hop Day!'
As crickets play their jazzy beats,
The garden dances, oh, it's sweet!

A squirrel steals a rose's crown,
Then winks as he runs 'round and 'round.
With petals soft and laughter loud,
This garden really draws a crowd!

Each blossom shares a witty pun,
As bees buzz in and join the fun.
In this bright world of giggles and grins,
Each day in bloom is where joy begins!

The Embrace of Heavenly Light

In sunlight's glow, we find our way,
Where flowers grin and children play.
The sunbeams waltz with cheerful flair,
As rain clouds grumble, not a care.

The daisies chuckle, full of cheer,
As rabbits hop and disappear.
An awkward dance of hips and tails,
Leaves the forest full of tales.

The clouds play peek-a-boo above,
While tree branches sway and shove.
A warm embrace from the skies bright,
As laughter echoes day and night.

Where butterflies boast about their flight,
And pixies giggle at their height.
In this embrace, we find delight,
Where all is funny, pure, and right!

Wandering the Realm of Bliss

In fields of fluff, where giggles grow,
The dandelions put on a show.
With each soft puff released with flair,
They whisper jokes into the air.

The path is lined with snickering stones,
And even bushes crack some bones.
As we meander with clumsy feet,
A race of worms can't be beat!

A sunflower grins, it's quite the sight,
Waving at us with all its might.
While ladybugs share stories grand,
Of adventures across the land.

With every step, the laughter rings,
And nature joins in with all its things.
In this realm of joy, we blissfully roam,
Finding our way, feeling right at home!

Melodies of the Twilight Orchard

Amidst the trees, I heard a tune,
A chipmunk swayed beneath the moon.
He danced with flair, oh what a sight,
A creature grooved with all his might.

The apples giggled, oh what fun,
They rolled around, just like they'd run.
A peach declared, 'I'm feeling bold!'
While cherries whispered tales of old.

The breeze it tickled every leaf,
With laughter shared, it brought relief.
"Let's skip the chores," the orchard said,
"Instead, let's feast on fruit and bread!"

In twilight glow, we danced along,
The critters joined us in a song.
With every strum, the world felt bright,
In this quaint orchard, sheer delight.

Roaming the Mosaic of Colors

Across the field, a rainbow blooms,
A squirrel jumps, with all his zooms.
The daisies wink, the poppies sneeze,
As butterflies fend off a breeze.

"There's magic here!" a ladybug cried,
"Let's paint the world, come take a ride!"
With splashes bright we'll color the air,
And giggle as we twirl without a care.

Bluebirds sing with cheeky glee,
While lizards dance beneath a tree.
A polka-dot frog hopped on by,
With tiny top hat and a big ol' sigh.

The sun got jealous of our fun,
And peeked through clouds, but we just spun!
With laughter echoing all around,
In this wild place, joy's surely found.

Under the Canopy of Hope

Beneath the leaves, we dared to dream,
Where acorns played in a silver stream.
A wise old owl gave her advice,
"Don't let your worries roll like dice!"

The squirrels chuckled, filling their cheeks,
With thoughts so grand, but not for weeks.
"Why plan ahead?" one exclaimed with joy,
"We'll celebrate now, every girl and boy!"

The shadows danced as the light did play,
While butterflies giggled, they swayed away.
A jolly breeze brought scents of pine,
As laughter twinkled like stars divine.

With every step, hope filled the air,
And worry fled, no time to spare.
Under this canopy of cheer,
We embraced the moment, year after year.

The Allure of Sun-Kissed Horizons

The golden sun set the sky ablaze,
While rabbits held their sunset craze.
They painted clouds with pink and gold,
And told the tales that never grow old.

The grasshoppers chirped a lively song,
While ants debated if they'd dance along.
A kitten pranced, not far away,
Belting out notes that made our day!

With every shadow growing tall,
A fox made plans for a grand ball.
"Ballet on the hill, let's show our moves!"
"See who trips! It's what the crowd loves!"

As twilight wrapped us in its glow,
We twirled and jumped with a flourish so.
With laughter echoing wide and far,
In sun-kissed dreams, we became the stars.

Wandering in the Fields of Light

In the fields where daisies dance,
I tripped and fell, not just by chance.
Bumblebees laughed as I went by,
Chasing butterflies that seemed to fly.

Under sunbeams, I did prance,
With ice cream drips, a sticky glance.
Hens were clucking 'bout my style,
"Is he crazy?" They'd quip and smile.

A squirrel stole my bright new hat,
To wear it, he looked quite the brat.
"Hey, return that!" I called in glee,
He winked at me, "It's a fashion spree!"

As the dusk wrapped in its soft embrace,
I saw the moon make a funny face.
In fields aglow, I spun around,
Joy in silliness, forever found.

Treading on Magic

On a path where pixies sneak,
I stumbled hard, out loud a squeak.
Mushrooms giggled, a funny sight,
"Can't you see? You're quite a fright!"

A rabbit hopped, so full of cheer,
"Join us now, but don't be near!"
He bounded off through tangled grass,
I followed quick, but let him pass.

Old oak trees whispered jokes so sly,
"Why do birds drink? To get a high!"
I chuckled loud, and then tripped low,
Fell on moss, the world a show.

With stars above, the night would tease,
Even crickets could laugh, if they please.
In whimsy realms where dreams take flight,
Who knew silly steps could feel so right?

A Stroll through Nature's Lullaby

In the woods, a lullaby hummed,
Leafy dancers twirled and thumped.
A raccoon jived with a funky style,
Cuffed my jeans, made me smile.

A brook babbled, "Can you keep pace?"
I leaped and splashed, saw the fish race.
"Hey there, friends!" I called in delight,
They flipped and dove, what a sight!

Clouds gathered like an old time band,
Strumming tunes from a far-off land.
With each step, I laughed and twirled,
Nature's stage, a funny world.

As twilight fell, owls gave a hoot,
"Got lost, did you? You silly brute!"
Under willows, with fireflies bright,
Silly giggles filled the night.

Exploration in Verdant Valleys

In a valley where green plants sway,
I tripped on roots, and then did play.
A goat nearby gave a knowing wink,
"Keep your balance, or you'll sink!"

Across the stream, a frog did croak,
"Hop on over! Here's the joke!"
As I leaped, made the splashy splash,
Frogs cheered me on, what a bash!

Kites soared high, caught in the breeze,
But mine got tangled in the trees.
The branches laughed, "You think you're grand?"
"Try to free it, that'll be unplanned!"

As dusk drew near, the stars took stage,
Even the moon flashed a funny page.
In valleys green, with giggles rife,
I danced in nature, embracing life.

A Tapestry Woven with Nature's Thread

In the meadow, I see a cow,
With a laugh, it says, "Moo, what now?"
Chasing butterflies, they flit and roam,
With buzzing bees who've lost their home.

Clouds drift by, with shapes absurd,
One looks like toast and another, a bird.
Even the trees are in on the play,
Their branches jiggle, come dance, they say!

A squirrel in a bowtie tries to impress,
Stealing nuts, then tripping, oh what a mess!
As I stroll through this nature-filled jest,
I can't help but chuckle, it's truly the best.

Beneath the sun's warm, cheeky grin,
I find joy in the silliness, deep within.
Every twist of fate, a laugh to share,
In this tapestry of life, I find flair.

Wondering Beneath the Celestial Canopy

Lifting my gaze to starry skies,
I swear I saw a comet wearing ties.
With laughter echoing on the breeze,
Even the moon wears a hat with ease.

Planets spin like tops, oh what a sight!
Venus does the cha-cha with all her might.
Saturn's rings are a giant snack,
What a cosmic party, no time to slack!

Shooting stars drop by for a chat,
Joking, "Catch me if you can! I'm flat!"
Galaxies giggle in spirals bright,
Twinkling secrets of the endless night.

I wonder if aliens join in the fun,
Trading their jokes while dancing 'round the sun.
Under this canopy, hilarity flows,
In the universe's embrace, joy only grows.

Vibrations of Color and Light

Pinks and purples dance in my sight,
They form a conga line, what a delight!
Green grass tickles my toes as I stroll,
While the yellow sun sings its glowing role.

Flowers wear costumes, each one a star,
Roses in tutus, daisies with guitars.
Bees buzz along, keeping perfect time,
With laughter and rhythm, nature's rhyme.

Bubbles of laughter float in the air,
Colorful ducks quack opinions to share.
A rainbow slips in, catapulting high,
It tumbles with glee, painting the sky.

In this carnival where giggles ignite,
Every hue sparkles with pure delight.
Vibrations of joy, a colorful spree,
Nature's palette brings such harmony.

In Search of Hidden Blossoms

In a garden of giggles, I tiptoe around,
Searching for blossoms that laugh, they abound.
One shout, "Pick me!" from behind the fence,
Another yells, "Stop! You're too intense!"

I find a daisy, with a wink and a grin,
It says, "Let's see who's the best at a spin!"
The tulips join in, twirling with flair,
While the violets gawk at the comical stare.

Pansies in pajamas play hide and seek,
Chasing the wind with laughter unique.
Every petal whispers secrets so sweet,
In this joyous patch, it's impossible to beat.

With each hidden blossom, a story unfolds,
Of mischief and pranks, a laughter that holds.
In search of these treasures, I find delight,
In nature's own comedy, sheer pure light.

A Pilgrimage Through Petal Dreams

Under candy clouds, I strolled with glee,
A squirrel in sunglasses, quite the sight to see.
Roses whispered secrets, daisies danced in flight,
A butterfly in a bowtie, pure delight!

The brook sang loud, it splashed with flair,
Fish in top hats, quite the aquatic affair.
Barking trees with laughter, branches waving free,
I giggled till I stumbled, oh, what a spree!

Gnomes played hopscotch on a mushroom mound,
While daisies held a party with confetti all around.
I claimed a prize—an acorn crowned in gold,
And shared my chips with a cat, a sight to behold!

So here's to frolics in the flowered jest,
Where laughter blooms above all the rest.
One step then another, what a silly jam,
In these petal dreams, I truly found my fam.

Colors in the Mist of Daybreak

Morning broke with giggles, hues all aflutter,
I stepped on a rainbow and slid in some butter.
Orange clouds did tango, purple trees did sway,
As a critter with a monocle shouted, "Hooray!"

Giggling dew drops rolled down sunny cheeks,
While snails in tutus practiced ballet leaks.
Fields of candy corn stretched as far as the eye,
With popcorn popping popcorn, oh my, oh my!

A gopher in a cape declared it was 'cheese,'
While bumblebees ate pancakes with ease.
Hats made of leaves were all the new craze,
And everyone danced in a syrupy haze!

So grab your balloons and twirl in the sun,
Where every silly moment is double the fun.
Colors in a mist, swirling with gleeful light,
In this whimsical realm, everything feels right!

Twilight Reflections of Eden

The sun dipped low, painting skies in gold,
As frogs in bowler hats told stories retold.
A river danced lazy, just looking for fun,
While fireflies played tag with the setting sun!

Mice wore pajamas, ready for a show,
While hedgehogs recited Shakespeare to a crow.
The grass whispered jokes, soft and so sly,
As the moon pulled up a chair, ready to try!

Crickets composed symphonies with flair,
And owls draped in scarves claimed the freshest air.
With every hush of twilight, laughter arose,
In a world that enchanted, where silliness flows!

So here in this glimmering, giggly abode,
Every glance brings smiles on this winding road.
Twilight reflects with a chaotic hue,
In this Eden of laughter, where dreams come true!

Journey Through Whimsical Foliage

Off I went through leaves dressed in polka dots,
Met a frog shaking maracas with funny thoughts.
Acorns threw a party, oh, what a ball,
As trees in wild wigs cheered, "Let's dance for all!"

Mushrooms wore capes, pretending to fly,
While vines told tales of a very bold guy.
A lizard in plaid offered jokes galore,
As twigs broke into laughter, begging for more!

The wind sang a tune that tickled my ear,
As flowers belt songs of joy, loud and clear.
Dandelions giggled, and wishes took flight,
On the whimsy express, everything felt right!

So here in this foliage, humor reigned supreme,
Where every little moment was a giggly dream.
This journey through laughter will never be done,
In the land of the silly, we're all number one!

Voyage Through the Lush Canopy

Swinging through the trees, oh what a sight,
Monkeys in hats, dancing with delight.
Parrots drop jokes, they're quite the tease,
While I trip on vines, saying, "I'm just here for cheese!"

Squirrels start rapping, trees join the beat,
They say, "Come on in, let's have a seat!"
Snack time arrives with a burst of surprise,
Coconuts fall, right onto my thighs!

Glimmers of sunlight sneak through the leaves,
Tickling my nose, oh how it weaves.
I'm dodging the branches with a silly grin,
Who knew nature's so wild? Let the fun begin!

At dusk, we toast to this crazy spree,
With fruits serving drinks, just wait and see!
As night blankets in with stars up above,
Nature winks, saying, "Here's my kind of love!"

Reflections in the Fountain of Love

At the fountain's edge, I see a fish,
Winking at me, granting my wish.
Soaked by a splash from a giddy child,
The laughter erupts, oh isn't it wild?

Ducks in tuxedos, they waddle in style,
Stealing the show, but they've got a great smile.
I toss a coin, but it lands on my shoe,
The fish just laughs, as if saying, "Boo hoo!"

Flowers nod gently, swaying to and fro,
Telling me secrets that I'd love to know.
But just as I lean in to gather their lore,
A butterfly lands, and I'm lost evermore!

As the sun sets down with a shimmering glow,
I leave with a laugh, feeling the flow.
With water and joy, it's the simplest shove,
Here in the splendor, I hand my heart, my love!

Dance of the Radiant Butterflies

Butterflies frolic, in colors so bright,
Like confetti thrown on a cold winter night.
They twirl and they spin, what a vibrant sight,
While I trip on daisies, oh, what a plight!

They float around, hosting their grand ball,
Whispering secrets as I trip and fall.
"Beware of the clumsy human below!"
They giggle and flutter, putting on a show!

Around the flowers, they swirl and glide,
As I try to join them, oh, what a ride!
Kicked dirt in my shoe, and I start to tread,
With each little twist, my face turns bright red!

But laughter leads me, as I tumble and spin,
A funny old waltz, oh, let's begin!
In the dance of the blooms, I find my wings,
Laughing with butterflies, oh, what joy it brings!

Journey to the Heart of Tranquility

Strolling through pathways where soft breezes sigh,
I ask a wise turtle, "How fast do you fly?"
He chuckles and says, "I'm quite on my way,
A little slow travel can brighten the day!"

Clouds start to gather, wearing fuzzy hats,
Before I can blink, they rain like splats!
Jumping on puddles, feeling carefree,
The world's a big joke, come laugh with me!

A warm breeze chuckles as it toys with my hair,
While ants stage a march, without any care.
They call out, "Hey human, come join our parade,"
And we stomp through the mud, a grand escapade!

Now the sun's dipping low, as day does retreat,
Mirthfully singing, we dance on our feet.
Wrapped in the laughter, my spirit is free,
This journey feels like a big comedy spree!

Serenity of the Emerald Walks

In emerald fields where daisies sprout,
I trip on my shoelace, oh what a clout!
The squirrels giggle, I can swear,
As I tumble down without a care.

Butterflies flirt with my flailing hair,
While singing birds laugh, but I just stare.
I dance like a potato, though I try to glide,
Nature must be laughing at my silly pride.

A rabbit hops by, with a curious peek,
I offer it snacks, but hey, I'm no freak!
We share in my lunch, and I swear it's true,
That bunnies have style, while I'm stuck like glue.

With each tiny step through the radiant maze,
I find myself lost in a comical daze.
The flowers all whisper, "You look quite absurd!"
But hey, I just smile, I'm the wackiest bird!

The Nectar of the Scented Breeze

In the garden of giggles, where aromas collide,
Bees buzz with laughter, I know they won't hide.
I sip on a nectar, a flower juice blend,
While bees tell me stories, my chuckles they send.

Daisies wear shades, looking fresh in the sun,
Roses roll their eyes, 'Oh, here comes the fun!'
A butterfly lands with a comedic flair,
He wiggles his wings like he hasn't a care.

The breeze takes my hat, in a whimsical swirl,
I chase it down paths, oh what a crazy whirl!
Flowers are snickering, as I dance in the chase,
With petals still giggling, I join the embrace.

A dandelion wishes, "Blow me a kiss!"
But I'd rather not try, it would end in pure bliss.
With laughter and giggles this garden will thrive,
For life is just better when absurdly alive!

Awakened by Nature's Breath

Awake to the sounds of a croaking frog choir,
With each ribbit, my laughter climbs higher.
A squirrel steals my sandwich, oh what a bold thief,
While I stifle my giggles, that's just beyond belief!

The sun tickles flowers, they sway in delight,
I join in their movements, my two left feet might.
As ants march in line, with a purpose so grand,
I stumble and fumble, the world's greatest band!

I wave to a tree, it waves back just as well,
"Come join our party!" it seems to yell.
But with branches above, I think I might fall,
Only laughter remains, in this floral brawl.

The wind blows a tickle, and I burst into giggles,
My hair's now a forest, just adding to wiggles.
Oh, nature's a friend, with her quirky flair,
In the land of the funny, I have not a care!

Pathways to the Heart of Beauty

Strolling through gardens, each path paved with fun,
With gnomes cracking jokes, under the bright sun.
I thought I saw beauty, but lo and behold,
It's just my reflection—quite awkward and bold!

Peonies whisper, "Why so much haste?"
I tiptoe in flowers, making humor my grace.
As bumblebees chuckle, conspiracies swirl,
I dance with the daisies, let laughter unfurl.

The sun paints my shadow, a silly charade,
I trip on a pebble, my senses betrayed.
But nothing can dampen this spirit of glee,
For every misstep leads to fun, can't you see?

With pathways of laughter and blooms all around,
I find joy in moments, where silliness is found.
In this garden of giggles, I'll always remain,
Where beauty dances lightly, and laughter's the gain!

Enigma of the Hidden Glade

In a glade where the squirrels do play,
They bounce and they chatter all day.
One stole my sandwich, oh what a claim,
In this forest, I've fallen for fame.

The flowers all giggle in their bright hue,
They tickle your nose, who knew?
A butterfly landed, with daring boast,
I asked for directions, but it just ghosted.

A frog in a bow tie, so proud and so grand,
Sings opera notes, isn't that quite planned?
He croaks a love song, makes my heart race,
But when he leaps off, oh what a disgrace!

I tripped over roots, with no one to see,
The trees all chuckled, oh, just let me be.
This glade of delights, so quirky and bright,
Is where laughter and nature unite!

The Symphony of Nature's Breath

The wind hums a tune through leaves on high,
While ants form a band, oh my, oh my!
They march in a row, quite out of beat,
But their tiny hearts dance to the rhythm sweet.

There's a crow with a top hat, who thinks he's a star,
He caws like a clarinet, oh, how bizarre!
The sun sets low, shining gold on the scene,
While crickets chirp jazz, in a musical sheen.

The brook bubbles laughter, splashes in glee,
"Catch a frog!" it whispers, "Come play with me!"
The fish wear sunglasses, they lounge by the shore,
While a snail's on a skateboard, but begs for more!

Nature's an orchestra, wild and unplanned,
With creatures who dance in a whimsical band.
So, join in their frolic, don't you delay,
The symphony's calling you, let's sway away!

Flourish Along the Blissful Path

Strolling along where the daisies cheer,
The dandelions whisper, "Come sit over here!"
A worm in a tux, gives a bow with a flip,
As I trip on a pebble, that slipped from my grip.

Bubbles of laughter, from flowers in bloom,
They're throwing a party, to lighten the gloom.
A chipmunk juggles, acorns held tight,
While I'm just here, trying to keep my shoes right.

The path sways and curves, like a dance on the grass,
With butterflies flitting, as quick as they pass.
"Caught you!" they giggle, "You've got no escape,"
And I chase after joy, like a comical drape.

With each step I take, I stumble and grin,
The world's but a stage, where the joy can begin.
Let's flourish together, in fun we'll be free,
In this madcap adventure, just you wait and see!

Harmonies in Nature's Embrace

In a world where the chickens recite poetry,
They peck at the words, oh what a sight to see!
A pig sings a ballad, with style and flair,
While ducks make a chorus, without a care.

The grass tickles toes, as I dance in delight,
With a squirrel doing breakdancing, such a sight!
A hedgehog in glasses, reads Shakespeare aloud,
While the trees sway to rhythms, oh how they're proud.

Beneath a wide sky, full of giggles and cheer,
The sun pops his head out, "Hey, it's all clear!"
While clouds play charades, in their fluffy old ways,
Every moment is magic, let's cherish these days.

So dance with the birds, let laughter arise,
In nature's embrace, under cobalt blue skies.
Life's surprisingly silly, it spins us around,
With harmonies bursting, in joy we are found!

Pathways of Infinite Wonder

Oh look, a squirrel in a hat,
Dancing with a chubby cat.
They twirl around the old oak tree,
Who knew they'd invite us for tea?

A flower bids me 'come play here,'
With polka dots, it whispers near.
A butterfly debates with a bee,
On who has the best cup of tea!

I trip on daisies with a grin,
And start a dance, it's a win-win!
A rabbit joins, all fluffy, spry,
Together we leap and touch the sky!

This path leads us to silly things,
Like mushrooms wearing tiny rings.
The sun peeks out, a friendly chap,
Invites us all to take a nap!

The Canvas of Nature's Whisper

A breeze whispers secrets in my ear,
Telling tales of bees with no fear.
Painted clouds in the sky so blue,
A canvas where dreams are made anew.

A wobbly hedgehog puffs with pride,
Rolling downhill, it goes for a ride.
Splashing through puddles, oh what a sight!
With every bounce, it takes flight!

Tulips gossip in colors bright,
Saying, 'Who wore that gown just right?'
A daffodil laughs with all its might,
As bees buzz by, a silly flight!

The grass tickles toes that dance,
Encouraging each and every chance.
Take a breath, and let out a cheer,
In this silly world, there's nothing to fear!

Glimpses Beyond the Golden Horizon

Beyond the hills, where sunlight bounces,
A family of ducks hilariously prounces.
They stomp in rhythm, quacking with glee,
Each step a dance, oh so carefree!

A sunbeam tickles the cheeky grass,
Where ants hold a dance-off, quite the class.
Each move they make, so bold and bright,
Makes even the flowers smile with delight!

A cloud floats by, with a "whoosh" and "pop,"
Daring the wind to give it a chop!
It puffs up larger, then starts to romp,
Engaging all critters in its bouncy chomp!

On this horizon, laughter spills,
From playful rabbits testing their skills.
Come join the fun, don't just stand there,
In this silly maze, there's joy to share!

Tales of the Vibrant Wildflowers

In fields of color, wildflowers sway,
Whispering secrets in a funny way.
One says, "I'm the prettiest here!"
While another bursts out with a giggle and cheer!

The daisies sunbathe, all stacked with grace,
While buttercups juggle in a wild chase.
A dandelion sneezes; uh-oh, oh dear,
Spreading wishes for all gathered near!

Caterpillars wear fashion, quite bold,
Strutting their stripes like stories untold.
Moths join in with a fluttering zest,
Creating a runway, it's a flower fest!

A wildflower band plays songs so sweet,
With bees buzzing along to the beat.
Nature's laughter is a vibrant sound,
In this garden, pure joy's found!

Serenade of the Seraphim

Oh, see the angels trying to sing,
While one forgot his pitch—what a thing!
They trip on clouds, their wings all a-flap,
With giggles and snorts, they take a nap.

With celestial cakes and lemonade,
They throw a party, and oh, what a parade!
Clouds become chairs, the stars play the flute,
Seraphim dance in their fuzzy old boots.

But look out below, here comes a wise owl,
Who shouts to the crowd with his best hoot and growl,
"Get off the grass, you fluffy-winged crew!
You'll ruin the garden, with feathers askew!"

So they gather their snacks, in hush, take a peek,
At the joyful scene where the flowers all squeak,
A serenade mixed with laughter and cheer,
Where even the squirrels join in with a beer.

Echoes of Enchanted Meadows

In meadows so bright where the daisies chat,
A cow tried to moo like a jazz acrobat.
With a top hat on and a bowtie so neat,
He swung with the breeze, tapping hooves to the beat.

Behind him the bunnies staged a ballet,
With pirouettes made of fine hay and clay.
But alas! Their grand leap sent them all flying,
Into pies of whipped cream, oh boy, how they're crying!

The butterflies giggle, their wings all a-flutter,
While snails wear the crowns made of sweet butter.
"Let's dance!" says the brook, with a splashing beat,
And frogs join the chorus—oh, isn't it sweet?

Yet up on a hill, the wise goats all stare,
"Stop all this ruckus, you're getting too rare!"
But down in the meadow, with laughter in tow,
The echoes of joy continue to flow.

Tranquil Trails Through Velvet Skies

Underneath the velvet stretch of the night,
Stars dressed in pajamas, oh what a sight!
They giggle and twinkle, play tag in the dark,
While comets whizz by, yelling, "Park it! Park!"

Clouds drift by softly, like cotton candy dreams,
Where starlings tell stories and giggle in teams.
"Did you hear about Lucy?" a star brightly quips,
"Her balloon went astray and gave the moon the slips!"

A bear on a tricycle zooms down the lane,
His hat made of cheese—he's a king with a reign!
With a roar of delight, he rides up to the stars,
"Hey, save me a slice! I'm coming, no cars!"

In this curious realm, where all worries cease,
Laughter drifts gently, it's pure joy and peace.
Beneath those soft skies, in such bliss we all dwell,
Where even the fireflies weave magical spells.

Harmony in the Orchard of Joy

In an orchard splashed with colorful fruit,
A dog once wore glasses, quite high-tech, to boot.
He gave advice on the best way to roll,
As apples fell, causing giggles to stroll.

The cherries had just started a band,
With plump little rhythms that were simply grand.
The pears played the drums with their funny round tums,
While grapes danced in cliques, making outlandish hums.

One peach was a joker, telling wild jokes,
While veggies all giggled, those punny old folks.
"Why did the tomato hide under a chair?
Because it saw the salad dressing and couldn't down stare!"

In this orchards' embrace, where laughter runs wild,
Nature's sweet symphony plays, heaven beguiled.
Together they flourish, with humor alight,
In a world where the sweet blends with funny delight.

Footsteps on the Rainbow Trail

In a land where unicorns play,
I tripped on a cloud, what a day!
Socks made of nachos, oh so neat,
Slipped right off my rainbow feet.

Lollipops grow on trees so sweet,
I made a new friend, a dancing beet.
We giggled as we bounced on mist,
Chasing after a chubby ghost twist.

Butterflies wearing hats of cheese,
Fluttered by as I sneezed with ease.
A parade of pufferfish swam by,
With jellybeans galore in the sky.

Clouds of cotton candy surprise,
Popcorn rain? Oh my, what a guise!
With each step, a silly prance,
In this world of gumdrop dance.

Blossoms of Serenity

In a garden where vegetables sing,
Carrots in tutus, what a thing!
Tomatoes giggled as they bloomed,
Squirrels in shades, swiftly zoomed.

Bees sipping honey like fine wine,
Baseball cap on a sunflower, divine!
Laughter echoed with each petal's sway,
As daisies played hopscotch all day.

A breeze like tickles in the air,
I found a fish wearing a chair.
Chasing a butterfly, it took flight,
Neon socks lighting up the night.

With every step, a comic twist,
Even the daisies couldn't resist.
Smiles all around, what a delight,
In this garden, everything's bright!

A Journey in the Cloak of Spring

In spring's jacket, oversized and grand,
I wandered through this funny land.
Hopping frogs in tuxedos jived,
As the daisies danced and thrived.

I bumped into a skunk with flair,
His bowtie made the flowers stare.
A cloud shaped like a silly cat,
Chasing down my big green hat!

Peacocks strutting with high-top shoes,
In a parade of polka dot hues.
Every step brought chuckles anew,
As I lost my way, but who knew?

I tangoed with a rainbow sprout,
While a hedgehog cheered me on, no doubt.
In spring's embrace, laughter was king,
What joy, oh what fun, this season brings!

Embracing Nature's Grace

Under trees that wear sunglasses bold,
I danced with squirrels, stories untold.
With grasshoppers playing the guitar,
I might just be a nature star!

A river of chocolate flowed right past,
I dove in with delight, what a blast!
A raccoon juggling with no care,
Dropped all his snacks everywhere!

The sun winks down with a goofy grin,
While frogs play hopscotch, let the fun begin!
A breeze tickles, I twirl and spin,
Nature's dance, where we all fit in.

With laughter echoing, we all unite,
In this whimsical world, everything's bright.
Embracing moments that sparkle and shine,
In nature's playground, life is divine!

The Serenity of Uncharted Realms

In a land where llamas wear shoes,
And trees whisper secrets of snooze,
Butterflies giggle, they flutter and dance,
While fish in green hats prance in a trance.

With clouds made of cotton and candy so sweet,
Sunflowers don sunglasses, can't handle the heat,
Chasing a rainbow that just won't sit still,
Oh, the joy of this place gives such a thrill!

Pineapples wearing snorkels dive in the air,
While turtles on surfboards show off their flair,
Each step is a chuckle, a twist and a shout,
In these realms where weirdness is what life's about!

So let's tumble along in this comical land,
With giggles, and wiggles, and magic so grand,
For laughter's the compass, it leads us with glee,
In the serenity only the silly can see.

Kaleidoscope of Dreams

Colors collide in a whimsical swirl,
Twirling like tops, oh what a whirl!
A frog in a tux with a top hat so fine,
Serenades daisies, 'You're simply divine!'

Banana peels slip in a jig on the ground,
Where squirrels in caps take the stage all around,
With popcorn-shaped clouds that pepper the blue,
Each laugh sets the scene, a spectacular view!

Jumping through puddles of sparkles and cheer,
A gopher in glasses looks wise and sincere,
He sips root beer floats, while jiggling about,
In this golden domain where silliness shouts!

So leap into wonder where giggles abound,
In this dreamscape of colors where joy can be found,
For each twist and turn makes the heart skip a beat,
In the kaleidoscope dreams, oh what a treat!

Serenity Along the Velvet Trail

Upon a soft path made of marshmallow fluff,
Where squirrels play chess and it's never too tough,
A turtle rolls by wearing bright neon socks,
While shadows dance lightly, like candy shop clocks.

Breezes hum tunes of a friendly old bear,
Who bakes silly cupcakes with sparkles to share,
On this trail, we skip; it feels liquid and light,
Waving to frogs in a jolly kite flight.

The trees wear bow ties, so sharp and so neat,
And owls in tweed suits discuss their next treat,
With laughter like bubbles that pop in the sun,
This velvet adventure has only begun!

So let's prance down this path with glee in our hearts,
Where the ordinary fades and the funny imparts,
For the moments of joy in the silliness reign,
In the serenity where whimsy unchained!

Dearest Delights of the Pastel Skies

Beneath skies so sweet, like a sugar-flecked dream,
Unicorns giggle with whipped cream on their seam,
Lollipops float by on a brisk cotton breeze,
While frogs in tutus dance fresh from the freeze.

Parrots tell stories, their feathers aflame,
Of mischief and puddles, and pranks gone the same,
Where pancakes tumble down from a fluffy white cloud,
And everyone cheers, joyous and loud!

In meadows of sprinkles, where daisies take flight,
The rabbits make puns, oh what a delight!
With each twist and turn through these pastel hideaways,
Life dances and twirls in the sunniest ways!

So let's frolic together in hues bright and gay,
In this land where the laughter is never passé,
For delights of the pastels, with each joyful sigh,
Make life taste so sweet—come join as we fly!

Essence of Untamed Freedom

With squirrels in capes that zoom and soar,
I chase my hat as it rolls on the floor.
The flowers gossip, whispering loud,
As bees form a band, they dance in a crowd.

The sun plays tag with the clouds above,
And ducks wear shades, oh how they shove!
The breeze tells jokes, it tickles my nose,
As I strut through this chaos, all laughter flows.

I trip on a root, do a clumsy twirl,
While butterflies giggle, in a fluttering swirl.
The grass is my sofa, the trees hold my drink,
In this wacky domain, where time starts to blink.

Life's a grand circus, and I'm the main act,
With a pie in my face as the audience clacked.
So I'll frolic forever in this bizarre spree,
'Cause who needs a map when you're wild and free?

Dance on the Leafy Breezes

The branches sway, I join their hip,
In a funky dance, I take a big trip.
Leaves are my partners, twirling hands,
While acorns laugh, forming dance bands.

I step on a snail; he's caught off guard,
He gives me a look like, 'Wow, that's hard!'
A squirrel throws down a feathered hat,
I wear it with pride, like 'Look at that!'

The daisies are bobbing; they want to groove,
But the wind gets jealous and starts to move.
So, we shimmy and shake, no rhythm to find,
As laughter erupts and hearts unwind.

A parade of misfits, all marching along,
With jingles of giggles that feel so strong.
I'll dance all day with my leafy friends,
Where the fun never stops and the laughter extends.

Gazing into Infinite Green

I peer through the foliage, a grand leafy sheet,
Where frogs play pianos and crickets tap feet.
The trees gossip secrets, their leaves all aflutter,
As the turtles discuss the latest nutter.

The clouds throw confetti as birds pass by,
Whispering jokes that make the owls cry.
The flowers nod politely, sipping their tea,
While lizards perform a slick two-step spree.

A butterfly stumbles, collides with my nose,
He spins in a dance; how silly it goes!
In this tapestry woven of laughter and cheer,
The giggles of nature just dance through the year.

I'm lost in this beauty, where nothing's routine,
With joy on the horizon, so bright and serene.
With every lost moment, a new giggle springs,
In this quirky green paradise, life sings and swings.

Around the Ever-Blooming Bend

I wander away from the well-trodden way,
Where flowers wear dresses of yellow and gray.
The bushes are gossiping, countless tales spun,
About ants in tuxedos, oh what a fun run!

There's a frog in a bow tie, he's calling the shots,
While caterpillars plan their grand polka dots.
The sun gives a wink, the clouds have a laugh,
As bees form a line for the sweet honey staff.

I trip on a daisy, it chuckles with glee,
And a bumblebee jives right next to me.
The grass is alive with its ticklish embrace,
Encouraging slips that I proudly face.

In this vibrant assembly of life's silly art,
I dance with the flowers, I know every part.
With laughter a-plenty and mischief in hand,
Around the ever-blooming, delightful we stand.

Ramble Beneath Radiant Canopies

Swaying branches with a teasing grin,
They poke at squirrels, trying to win.
A chubby raccoon smirks at the fuss,
Playing hide and seek on the green bus.

Beneath the leaves, a shadowy joke,
A frog sings loudly, sounding like smoke.
The flowers giggle in matching hues,
As butterflies dance in crazy shoes.

A wise old owl chuckles above,
Watching antics, a wild, silly love.
The ants are marching in mismatched lines,
Dreaming of picnics and endless fines.

So off I skip, with a wink and a nod,
In this leafy realm where the goofy plod.
With each step, laughter sprinkles about,
Nature's own jest in this joyous route.

Nature's Breath Under the Starlit Arch

Twinkling lights above, the stars all chat,
A raccoon passes by wearing a hat.
He bows politely then prances away,
Giggles erupt through the night's ballet.

Crickets compose a wacky tune,
Singing in harmony, left none too soon.
A dog howls back, a vocal refrain,
Together they dance, both silly and insane.

Moonbeams snippet a shimmering joke,
As fireflies flicker, in unison stoke.
With every glimmer, a laugh does appear,
Nature's own jesters, we hold so dear.

So stroll along this shimmering sea,
Where giggles and whispers are wild and free.
Under the arch where the stars like to play,
Laughter abounds at the end of the day.

The Hush of Afternoon Delights

In the shade of an oak, I pause to snack,
While ants conspire—what's their master plan, Jack?
They tickle my toes with their march so grand,
I can't help but chuckle at their tiny band.

A chipmunk giggles, then makes a bold leap,
While butterflies flutter in a parade so deep.
A lizard sunbathes, his grin a bright smile,
Daring the sun to stay a while.

The breeze whispers secrets, a playful tease,
As daisies sway gently—dancing with ease.
I spot a gopher trying to dig a new home,
But his butt keeps popping out like a silly gnome.

The sun dips low, painting laughter in gold,
As shadows do jiggles, both funny and bold.
In the hush of the day, where jokes find their flight,
Afternoon delights fill the air with pure light.

Medley of Morning Glories

Morning arises with a wink and a giggle,
While roosters crow in an offbeat wriggle.
The sun yawns loudly, stretching its beams,
And pink clouds dance, bursting at the seams.

Squirrels argue over the best acorn,
While dew drops twinkle, a jewel adorned.
A bunny hops past in a parade of cheer,
With a floppy-eared hat that's fashion severe.

The flowers wake up, all ready to play,
And tickle each other, in bloom's ballet.
With colors so bright and smiles in-store,
They salsa and cha-cha, an Instagram score.

As buzz of the bees fills the morning air,
They've brought tiny jokes, oh so delightful to share.
With each tiny chuckle, the day finds its groove,
In this morning symphony, let's dance and move!

Clusters of Joy in Every Step

With each little hop, I search for a prize,
A candy-wrapped treasure—much to my surprise!
The flowers all giggle, they nod and they sway,
As I dance with the bugs, who want to join play.

The squirrels are gossiping under a tree,
They whisper sweet secrets about pastry and tea.
My shoes start to squeak as I leap over roots,
Do they join in the laughter, or just mock my boots?

The sun throws confetti while I skip along,
The shadows behind me join in with a song.
A puddle does wink, reflecting my glee,
As if it's a mirror, oh look, that's just me!

Oh, joy is contagious, it's caught like a sneeze,
A tickle of laughter floats by on the breeze.
With clusters of fun, I can't help but smile,
No frown can survive in this whimsical mile.

Visions Beneath the Celestial Canopy

Under this vast blanket of stars shining bright,
I ponder my choices with cookies and sprites.
An owl gives a hoot, not a care in the world,
His wisdom is scattered, like leaves, it's unfurled.

A rabbit named Waffle hops over my foot,
He offers me pastries while munching on fruit.
"Join me!" he exclaims, with a flick of his ear,
The celestial show is magic quite near!

I stumble on stardust, trip over the moon,
Waffle just giggles, "You'll learn it quite soon!"
The night sky is winking, it knows all the jokes,
As I chuckle with constellations and folks.

With visions so vivid beneath this vast dome,
Every twinkling star feels just like coming home.
I sweep up the laughter like fireflies catch,
In this lovely night's glow, no soul feels unmatched.

Unfolding the Scrolls of Bliss

A map of delight rolls out in the sun,
Every line is a giggle, a riddle of fun.
I follow the arrows, they point to good cheer,
With snacks along the way, I have nothing to fear.

The fountain's quite chatty, it bubbles with glee,
As ducks waddle past, pretending to be free.
"Are we lost or just wandering?" they ponder aloud,
"All I see is cake—hey, we're feeling quite proud!"

I open a scroll made of giggles and grins,
A treasure that's hidden in laughter begins.
With every small crinkle, a laugh waits inside,
Each fold a reminder where chuckles abide.

In this realm of pure candy, joy floats like a kite,
From the skies fall delight, as day dances with night.
With scrolls of euphoria, we scribble our dreams,
Life's tricks and its treats are more fun than they seem!

Wonders Beneath the Tree of Life

Under the wise branches, I pause to connect,
With a cheeky old squirrel who sure has respect.
He offers his wisdom in acorns and nuts,
While pigeons discuss, "Well, who really struts?"

The roots of this tree twist like taffy so sweet,
I can't help but laugh as I try to take a seat.
A parrot swings by, "What's the news, my dear friend?"
With colors so bright, his gossip won't end.

Each rustle and giggle makes magic unfold,
With wonders aplenty, both precious and bold.
The sun throws a party of glorious rays,
As nature rejoices in silly ballet.

Under this vibrant tree, let the laughter take flight,
With joy as my compass, I'll dance through the night.
For every soft whisper and chuckle I find,
The wonders of living are perfectly intertwined.

Steps Among the Blossoms

With flowers like hats, they wave and cheer,
I swear they're gossiping, oh dear, oh dear!
A bee buzzes by, with a sass so grand,
It steals my snack; how rude, I planned!

A butterfly flutters, dressed to impress,
Calls out to the ants, 'You're a total mess!'
They giggle and dance, in their tiny shoes,
While I just trip over my own two blues.

The sun's a jester, with warming rays,
It tickles my nose in mischievous ways.
Each step feels like fun on a carnival ride,
With giggles and squeaks, come join the tide!

I stumble upon a patch of mud,
Oh look! I've twisted like a fun-filled thud.
While daisies laugh, so bright and spry,
I'm just a clumsy fool, oh my, oh my!

Serenade of the Radiant Path

On a pathway paved with petals bright,
Sunbeams laugh with the clouds in flight.
A squirrel poofs up, all bristled and bold,
Stealing my sandwich, so brazen, so cold!

The trees gossip, their branches a-mingle,
"He tried to dance, but he stumbled and jingled!"
A flower winks, and pollen pops,
As I chase a breeze, my sanity drops.

A bird thinks it's wise, starts singing flat,
But I tap my toes, and it thinks I'm a brat!
With giggles all around, nature holds court,
As I juggle my snacks with a fanciful sort!

Down the lane, where the lilies sway,
I trip on a root, "Hold my tea!" I say.
This rhythm of chaos, in petals and cheer,
In a whole world of giggles, I twirl without fear!

Journey Through Eden's Embrace

In a field where the daisies play hide and seek,
I trip on a vine with an ungrateful squeak.
A snicker from petals, oh who could it be?
Is that laughter from grass, or just lil' old me?

The sun wears sunglasses, looks quite the dude,
While shadows sneak in, they're plotting, how rude!
A parade of ants, with tiny drums bang,
March not to my feet, with a chorus I sang!

Past the tulips, a breeze gives a tickle,
I crack up and giggle, it's quite the riddle.
Mysteries bloom, like the pranks of a sprite,
"Why's the garden so funny?" I laugh with delight!

With nature as funny as a stand-up show,
I'll keep on my journey, just taking it slow.
And if the squirrels mock, I'll join in the jokes,
In this Eden of laughter, where joy always pokes!

The Lush Voyage

Set sail on the grass, oh what a view,
Where daisies are captains and clouds hold the crew!
A frog in a hat, croaks out a tune,
While bees do the cha-cha, beneath the bright moon.

The paths twist and turn, like a dance of delight,
As I dodge falling acorns that drop from great heights.
A robin cracks jokes, with a wink and a cheer,
While mushrooms pop in, just to lend me an ear!

Oh, a raspberry bush offers me a treat,
One bite, and I'm flourished with berry-sweet heat!
The bushes tease me, "You can't handle the zest!"
With laughter, I munch, feeling truly the best!

A swirl of the petals, a tumble, a spin,
As I roll with the flowers, let the fun times begin!
With each rosy scent, like a giggle on air,
In the lushest of journeys, who needs to beware?

A Voyage Among Celestial Blooms

Floating in a sea of bright blooms,
Bees wear tiny hats, making their rooms.
Wobbly petals dance in the breeze,
Bumblebees giggle, oh what a tease!

Butterflies park on daisies so wide,
While ladybugs gossip, full of pride.
The sun delivers its warmest jive,
As flowers plot schemes to keep bees alive.

Roses argue with daisies for fun,
Snapping selfies 'til the day is done.
A garden party, the wildest show,
With worms dressed up in their finest bow.

A rainbow arches, a backdrop bright,
As spinach serenades under starlight.
Frogs in tuxedos sing, "What a sight!"
In celestial blooms, joy feels so right!

The Allureness of Sun-Drenched Hills

The rolling hills wear their sunny hats,
Squirrels snicker, oh such silly brats!
Napping bunnies get startled awake,
By daisies who joke, "Let's have a cake!"

Cows in shades sip lemonade so cool,
While ducks quack secrets in the pool.
Over the hill, a prankster goat,
Surprises a sheep with a wild note.

The sun beams down, a glorious wink,
As flowers sip coffee, and cats think.
A parade of ants march with glee,
"Who said hills aren't the best place to be?"

With laughter and joy in the air,
Every nook has its quirks of fair.
As the sun dips low, the night unfolds,
These sun-drenched hills hold laughter like gold!

Moments in the Timeless Meadow

In a meadow where time does a silly dance,
Grasshoppers volley, glancing askance.
The daisies debate, who's the best bloom,
While butterflies ponder, "What's with the gloom?"

An ant dreams big, with plans for a throne,
As a thoughtful worm jots notes in the stone.
Clouds above lounge, sipping their tea,
While rabbits play hopscotch, oh what a spree!

A kite caught on a breeze takes its flight,
Chasing after dreams and thoughts of delight.
The sun gives high-fives to each blooming sprout,
As nature's humor keeps the fun about.

Just a waltz in the grass, under skies so blue,
Where laughter and whimsy grow on each dew.
Moments like these make hearts skip a beat,
In the timeless meadow, life's ever sweet!

Lush Oases of Wonder

In lush oases where giggles sprout,
Cactus wiggle while shouting, "We're out!"
Palms play hide and seek with the sun,
While meerkats debate who's most fun.

A fountain of chocolate, what a delight,
With sprinkles and laughter that sparkles at night.
The parrots squawk jokes in vivid hues,
As camels sip smoothies, just catching the views.

Sandcastles tower, their flags in the air,
Crabs in tuxedos entertain with flair.
Every corner brings giggles and cheer,
In oases lush, fun blossoms here!

Smoothie sandstorms swirl, and laughter won't cease,
With fruits and delights, all bloomin' in peace.
In this haven of wonder, we prance and we zip,
Creating our memories, on a laughter trip!

www.ingramcontent.com/pod-product-compliance
Lightning Source LLC
Chambersburg PA
CBHW072118070526
44585CB00016B/1491